Out

MW01274571

Out of Time, Running

Edward Nudelman

Harbor Mountain Press
Brownsville, Vermont

Harbor Mountain Press, Inc., is a 501(c)(3) organization
dedicated to works of high literary merit. Harbor
Mountain Press books are distributed nationally
and internationally through Small Press Distribution,
a non-profit organization (spdbooks.org) in Berkeley,
CA, as well as by the GenPop book consortium and
through fine local bookstores. Harbor Mountain Press
appreciates support from individual donors, via Net-
work for Good, and from the generosity of grant giving
organizations concerned with arts, literacy and culture.
Please help us build an endowment.

Series Editor, Director
Peter Money

Design
Bryan Stone

Cover art from sculptures by Ernest Montenegro,
used with permission of the artist.
ernestmontenegro.com

Harbor Mountain Press
P.O. Box 519
Brownsville, Vermont
o 5 o 3 7

Acknowledgments

Grateful acknowledgment is made to the editors of the journals and anthologies who first published the following poems, sometimes in earlier versions, as follows:

Cortland Review, "From a Car, Gazing at My Boyhood House"

Evergreen Review, "Famous Numbers, And Then There's Me"

Lummox Magazine, "Lizard Status"

Mipoesias Magazine, "November," "Death By Pastel," "A Modern Surrender"

Poets and Artists, "Forfeit," "Disco Cool"

Valparaiso Review, "Photo"

for Laurel
who has endured so much
and yet keeps running

Table of Contents

III.

I.

Melody of Complaint

Blue fall of night, stillness
behind an eye. In the fifteenth
hour I stop invoking selfhood
and splay Byron on his spine.
Faith would warm my hands
if I had it, and doubt would hog
the room if I let it, but my mood
shrinks this house into a cell.
Here is where I leave my wants
and wills. A stack of papers,
a desk riddled with sheets
and letters and numbers.
Above the bookcase leaded
with broken glass, tulips
in a glass jar begging for light.
Everything, as it were,
begging for light.

Biochemist in a Cold Room

Backlit droplets fall single-file
into one of two-hundred tubes.
I move them with absent fingers.
I move them to catch the glinting.
Impossible tasks feed damp air
straddling dipole and charge,
and I a frozen line of urgency
which is my solemn inheritance.
Each shivering microliter bifurcates
equal parts myth and discovery.
Each possibility creeps forward
and slides backwards
on serendipity's smooth ice.
It's a good thing I'm here
in the middle of the night
when the error of judgment
is less pronounced, when artifact
more easily passes for breakthrough.
Any way I look at this, the same
answer crystallizes, teasing out a gray
moon to wash an unlit night.

From a Car, Gazing at My Boyhood House

I think I see my bedroom's peeling wallpaper,
the gaps around my bed, long penned notes
to Lynnette and later Marla. I hear the night's
creepy hush interrupted by my alarm clock's
sticking second-hand, feel my stocking-clad
feet gliding over cold slate, fingers grasping
the refrigerator door for balance. My mother
and father ghost the stair landing. She's lipping
a burned-out cigarette and he's on two boxes
wresting a light bulb from the broken socket.

Id-Ridden

I don't have to go far into the day
before I lose a clear sense of who I am.
I seem to be fading into the background
while countless unrecognizable me's
creep forward in stealth, wearing hats
and gray overcoats. They sit down with me
at night, share my silverware and keep
conversation with alien life forms.
It's taken me so long to figure out
I'm right-brained, that it's almost too
late to make use of the revelation.
But perhaps it's better that way,
not knowing the real you, let it somehow
slip out between the lines, as they say,
though I've never found anything
between the lines but blank space.

I Need Trees

I need their birds
and dampened bark.
I need their loud swift
jingling and I need
their rare composure
over this moving
raucous house. I need
every angle triangulated,
every lean and turn
fully integrated.
My stilted speech
wavers hallelujahs
among their branches.

Pilot Comedy

The comic still surfaces
against all odds, even after
years of quiet dwindling.
She laughs at the TV
and little children,
all her near falls and fits.
But not funny if her dog
isn't fed or put out to pee.
And not funny if windows
are left open in winter;
or breakfast without sugar.
Not funny, losing grip
of a fork, a thought,
the hand railing.
Every random asteroid
in her variegated universe
seems to circle overhead
without gravity;
stars, moons and comets
holding vigil like bad
jokesters in a silent room.

Electron Spin

The mind's split screen plays double
feature: sun blurring like an orbital,
moon off to sulk in its cloud room.
And I'm supposed to sit here
and be quiet, obey the commands
from the stars and silky shadows?
I'm counting the vibrations with my toes
on telephone wires stretched like guitar
strings across a narrow opening.
What I hear is the probability of sound.
I strum the raw progression
over my head's blue electronic hiss.
A raven has its way with the wind.
A black hill bisects its own shadow.
The wind hammers like a howl.
The sea is rising, rising, rising.
Bit by bit I forge a temporary truce
through the day's war and waste.
Plusses and minuses, zeroes and ones,
a school of hungry fish swimming behind.

View From Goat Hill

One remembers only the essentials:
burnt grass, scruffy oaks with paper
brown leaves, horizon with water birds
beaded, and the eye's camera panning
every crooked angle: from the school's
drooping gargoyles to the narrow inlet
and the boatless ocean like silver slate.
A few lights beam out from gray hills
across the bay, sound of phantom foot
traffic on streets marked by the same
unmovable fogbank, the same hush.

Western Dream

Paper shover,
pot-hole filler, iridescent
bird of the gray night.
You are the embodiment
of body sans soul,
the next bad bandito.
Dream hoverer, self-hewer,
masked man on a horse
from Cheyenne
and the burning hills.
All day without water
and still it is a paper
cut that causes pain.
All summer long
on the plateau
looking for green,
and still the engine
roars above the canyon.
The sun rises boldly
on your sunglasses,
ricocheting like a bullet.

Greater Loss

The dying ant clings
to a dying ant,
the sheep to her sacrifice.
She bleats for it in a green
field or steamy abattoir.
A blot or a mote, a mouse
on its retrograde motion
back to its starless
night under the staircase.
The measure of success
down here among the reeds
and blades, is it not the
divergence of life?
Can one discern a single
dot in a sea of pixels,
a discrete cloud
over darkening skies?
I heard a lone voice
crying in the wilderness.
I saw an ant lumbering.

Poem That Stands On One Leaf

In such a way that trees shake
in order to catalyze unweighting.
Not that one is more than many,
except in extreme circumstances–
such as when a barn begins to fall
plank upon plank on an uphill road
garnering compliments from us all
zooming by with camera phones.
One becomes used to a leg,
and its absence creates problems.
But when both a leg and arm drop
off, the embarrassment is palpable.
Some say the human mind adapts
to both physical and emotional
loss in similar ways. Some say
it doesn't matter how you think,
the day still gives way to night.
The oak hollows by degree after
all these years animated, and nobody
notices any decline until one
Sunday afternoon, under threatening
skies and a stiff wind, it buckles,
while the poem moves forward,
balancing on its good leg.

Photo

My father's cigar
burned down to the label
in southern France
on a tarmac
between the waging
of poker and war.

Early Walk in a Strange City

From tangled sheets you wrest free
while others sleep, propelling bone
and neuron through dawn's luster.
You slither forth like snake,
calling out dark by its secret names,
one by one, from steaming manholes.
Your fevered empires peel back,
white blood cells arm and load,
breaking chemical bonds.
In the space of four square blocks
you've solved more problems
than you knew existed,
all before orange juice and toast.
But as the streets begin to fill,
you slink back on cat's feet
and take your place in the pinball
world you've made comfortably
tolerable. A room two flights up
with one door, one chair, one light bulb
and one more transient life form
tapping patiently with knife and fork.

November

Solid shape and contoured space we seek,
void with void's ineluctable pattern; unit,
scale, breadth, distance. What we need:
contrast, discernment, a way through noise.
An egret bent over backwards, her neck
a ruffle of splayed gray feathers, another
landing close by; the pond a target
nature aims its arrows at. Hear the distant
beginning of an argument sending
its plundering army, as winter stitches
one bare branch to another, one shovel
full of leaves upon the next, burying
the dormant larvae in its hardened bed.

Hundred Trillion

Ten to the fourteenth power, which
is about a tenth the number of ants
crawling on the earth at any one time.
It's how many cells are in your body,
(but 90 percent of those are bacteria).
Any attempts at counting to a hundred
trillion will end in failure. I once sat
alone and tried to count to a billion.
This became difficult at two thousand.
A hundred trillion is the number
of times it would take to randomly
throw up a million letters and have
them float to earth and write out
a complete Shakespearean sonnet.
But this would leave many left over,
which could be used for other poems.

II.

The Life of Riley

Invoked between
office back-stabs
and hammock-tipping
on a warm evening
back in the safe confines.
The air was dark and thick
and gritty; now in paradise
it breathes lilac and magnolia.
A little caveat goes a long way.
As does excess and the surfeit
of pleasure and comfort.
Little moth on a light bulb,
how much is too much?

Monk Inside

I picked up a newspaper tonight,
discovered who we are and where
we're going, in three turgid
paragraphs, a didactic splurge.
This is a benefit for all mankind,
a harrowing near-miss down
the worm hole of inconsequentiality.
And to think I've immersed myself
four decades in the code of it,
sold out on good days and succumbed
on bad days to the hierarchy of genius.
Scientist, mud-god, skunk of wisdom,
articulate sage beyond shadow, omnivore
of earth and cloud, speak to me no more
in your native tongue of secrets
unblanketed, of riddles unraveled.
Restless I am for the lapping moon
and the first birds of the morning,
in my fiftieth year of fasting and prayer.

Kate's Room

I am sitting in a room that once hosted an infant,
trying to abstract from a basket full of concrete.
It is a brute fact that slays apprehension,
the sweet sound of a babe cooing nearby.
I am sitting in a room extracting sugar from a jar
of jelly beans and I'm almost done with today's
cruel work. How did I get from here to there
with both limbs and legs and reasonable brain intact?
It's probably no accident that the pine walls
are now hidden by pine bookcases, and those
nearly filled with a library of levant and morocco.
If I close my eyes and lift my chin up high
I can easily smell the tinny, sweet odor
of the bee's nest that grew behind your
closet (which we all thought smelled like pot).
If I raise my arms high enough, I can imagine
how the seraphs slept beside you, bearing witness.
Who says the walls don't talk? I am listening.

Thou Shalt Overcome

Sightlines of anticipation
staring down the demon's
demon with a mouth full
of chewing gum. Lactic
acid spilled on the floor,
bone on bone, the wheels
turning. Suffice it to say,
you'd bear it all for one
good night's sleep. Lying
back unabashed, cleared
from its melodrama,
reflecting the full measure
of upheaval sustained,
you gently profess
echoing the prophet, *Selah*;
all through the night's
dark temple; *Selah* to the owl's
solitary hoot and the grim
grinding of distant engines.

Tunisia

Softly she floats on a bed of dreams.
Outside the pear trees seem to over-bloom,
and the walkway is a brilliant grass rectangle.
She tells me she is in Tunisia or Turkey.
She explains everything quite logically,
from heated sands to hissing sidewinders.
The food is bad, but she keeps the leftovers
in a small plastic cup, a few grapes, some yogurt
with half a hard-boiled egg balanced on top.
She wants out of the desert, and she wills
this through a combination of familiar words
and relentless rivers of consciousness.
Outside, men and women come and go
with greetings and salutations. Inside, clouds
part over room three. Hot air rising over
cool air produces waves. So too, a mirage
and a pebble entering a calm blue lake.

A Modern Surrender

A long walk in December, militia
and murderers notwithstanding.
The weather slakes after ruinous binge.
You don't have to take everything
so seriously, she says, in front of her statue.
A bunch of red birds pecking snow
from a torn postcard mailed from
one kingdom to a another, a heartbreak
sculpture in every way.
Is it possible to survive two lives?
The wind complains like a querulous
monarch. Wing to wing on a wire,
the birds croak. *Off with their heads*.

Longevity

Aging faces greet me inaudibly,
but they come with ulterior motives
and second messengers.
Pinholes in my head, fault lines
from which the brain escapes,
atom by atom, until the last thought
finds a gaping breezeway.
What's now left to interest me,
of sun spots, moon craters or cities
I'll never visit or dream about?
I'm on the road with neither hands
nor feet in working order.
It's not that I don't like this life.
The winds at night frighten me
into a deep and solemn sleep,
the birds in the morning fill my soul.
Take me then or take me now,
before shade blights the lawn,
before the old forest thins.

Subatomic Rambling

Bosons obey Bose–Einstein statistics
and hence can occupy the same
quantum state, while fermions
have half-integer spin and tend
to actively associate with matter.
Gravitons are hypothetical particles
which seem to mediate gravitation.
If you swap two fermions, the wave
function of the system changes.
As far as I'm aware, I have no
functioning wave or measurable spin.
When I sleep, my eyes dance in C minor
and my ears hear the oak trees grow.

Death by Pastel

Next, the dog-haired wheeze, merciless
bellow from sleep, trumping stillness.
Agonist and comforter meshed as one,
circumnavigating relief. Eyes strain,
ears peel into walled unknowabilty.
Easy to cough in a room full of smoke,
far less facile to keep this uproar going
in dustless white of night; chest muscles
unhinged, hobgoblins rising up in bins
and treasures, the long since dormant
hope-slayer, your voice box's jingling
jangle, deified into symbol and song.
Moving forward and upward in the pale
skin-colored air, come nocturnal
animals, blind and pink. Now and then
soft tones overwhelm the gritty gray.

Passing the Bar

This is the greatest moment of my thirteen years of life.
So it began, though I can't remember how it ended:
my Bar Mitzvah speech had something to do with going
into the land of milk and honey (my father wrote it).
He coached me well on its delivery, when to pause,
when to raise and lower my voice, and when to stop
altogether, looking slowly look up for what he termed
the palpable pause. If I did anything well in that speech
it was at those moments, peering out from my yamaka
with marbled eyes, tilting my head a bit sideways,
ever-pressing the envelope of suspenseful melodrama.
Afterwards, following much hoopla, the rabbi explained
I had omitted two lines from a key prayer, henceforth
casting my manhood precariously in the balance.

Fever

Night eclipsing night. Cue avarice
beast, cue hammer and tongs and rhyming
refrain. Let not the dregs of heaven forestall
the inevitable geothermal event; let not
oil or crystal stymie the advancing horde.
Cue scotch and port and bergamot,
loathsome blend of lemon peel and rind.
Four eyes, then eight, a hundred yellow
spheres rolling down from the hills.
On the portico, dazzling fires snorting
through glazed eyes and charred nostrils.
A plethora of all-consuming.

Forfeit

Love and hate share the same minor chord.
Love employs the tongue but hate rails
wordlessly from the back of the throat.
She bore her love in the same room
her pain meandered, her child
in the same air grayed by cohabitation,
heavy particles weighing down the will.
When one army fell back, another rose up.
When one skin peeled, another
filled in, massive and scaly.
It's no wonder the heart
lags so far behind the mind.
Love quickens, but so does hate.
Both begin at the end, then move inward.
She called her hate a deafening noise;
her pain, when she could feel it,
a muffling wind through trees.
And one day she looked down to find
arms wrapped in ice and both feet
inserted into cement blocks.
It is hard carrying you around inside
of me, she used to say to her belly,
and the noise of it built itself into a refrain
and then a song splayed across an orphan breath.

Lizard Status

In this shifting habitat, released from every creeping
companion, I stop projecting incipient outcomes,
stop receiving imposters and grown apes at my doorstep.
On dry sand perfectly unveiled, skewered by every
rod of blessing, here am I: unbridled brine, these lofty
thoughts of grandiose, these red line notes. Incline to me
wizards of thin air, carrier gulls with your glamour news
and harbinger signs. Three nights, three days in the desert
nictitating each verse peddled under the unbarred sun.
Here am I, coming to rest on linen. A pear. A cleanly
manicured sardine sandwich, all the blistering this world
can afford. Bring it on, singe and scar; hail inalienable rights
and white-hot silica. O gutting pain, O heat of exultation.

Taking Down a Roof

Not everyone gets the chance to do it,
but if you get lucky, I recommend the roof
with asbestos-type shingles, discovered
a couple weeks into the job. Not that we
didn't suspect asbestos, it's just the kind
of detail you don't vocalize, even to your
partner of so many years, so many shared
experiences, so many crowning zeniths.
And how many actual fibers constitute
a risk... fourteen, a thousand, ten million?
Then there's the equation of justification
versus rationalization; not really an equation
but a null set. Therefore, let x be the asbestos
shingle. Let y represent the total number
of asbestos atoms on any given shingle.
Let m be the inhalation quotient through
a qualified mask; and finally, let r be
the probability of acquiring mesolthelioma.
Then, let yourself down carefully from
the ladder which doesn't have a bottom
rung and rests partly in a flower bed
and partly in the abstract room
of human endeavor, somewhere
between heroism and outright idiocy.

Dad's Luger

I think I explored father's side of my parents' walk in closet
more than I explored the deep forested ravine a few blocks away.
On my mother's side were mothballs and hats, cellophane-dressed
evening gowns, mounds and mounds of shoes. But my father's side
had guns and ammo, tobacco, boxes of chocolate bars and a huge
silver treasure chest which was actually filled with silver and gold.
He never caught me stealing his revolver nor had any inkling
of me unloading six shells into the bark of our madrona tree.
He never knew how regularly I reduced his supply of chocolate
and he never knew I rolled my first cigarette around his musty old
tobacco that smelled like skunk. Though one day he came home
early and found me and Kent Bollenbach on their king size bed
with every shining coin spread out and organized by date.
After that, the chest was sealed with a double-sized padlock,
and the tobacco and chocolate were nowhere to be found.
However, the luger remained in its place on top of a box of luger
bullets; and his story of prying it out from the hands of a dead
Kraut still dutifully raised eyebrows and the hair on my boyish neck.

Lab Accident

Biochemists are like babies, inquisitive and balding, emit
funny sounds and complain whenever possible. Importantly,
they err without grace and frequently. One day, when
lilacs bloomed, I homogenized my index finger just after
a hearty lunch, near the roto-evaporator. The industrial-sized
blender was loaded with caustic solvents and human tumors.
Beth, the over-reactive lab tech with scarlet hair possessing
a pretty decent falsetto and Kiyotoshi Miramoto, MD/PhD
(who couldn't speak one word of English) both ran screaming
into the hall while I felt my way to the eyewash like a newt.
Kiyo finally came back with a fire extinguisher and Beth
with a towel. Blood filled the sink as I imagined my eyeballs
swirling down the drain. Later that night I enjoyed ice cream
and tortilla chips, managing to stay awake long enough
to catch the restaurant scene in Good Fellas. Back in the lab
the next morning, subtle innuendos and bad jokes started early.
Still, I wielded my P-200 Gilson Automatic Pipettor with
semi-automatic action via my good left hand, drawing up
75 microliters of phosphate buffered saline and emptying it
delicately into the bottomless well of my chagrin.

Reflecting Death

I don't see my loved-ones
gathering around photos
and reveling over good times.
I don't hear sparkling eulogies
or trumpets blasting out a refrain.
Just my dog Sofie, asleep at the door,
barking at my every ghostly breath,
awaiting my return with her orders
and requests and endless chides.
Or am I being overly sentimental?

III.

Four Maxims for the Bereaved

It is better to share your grief with a pod of whales than swim
around in a bowl of heartless goldfish.

Good things happen to bad people and bad things happen
to good people; on the other hand, a mountain never has
a birthday party and a computer never cries.

Dwelling on the past is not only an art form, it is an epic
movie we watch every night before falling asleep.

What's ironic about grief is that it never fully goes away,
and that's what makes it tolerable.

Wordless Refrain

Today my wife wistfully declared
she couldn't spell the word wow,
a confession for the ages, until I
disclosed my failure to spell P.U.
Fissures in our otherwise smooth
thought terrain; trivial at times,
but an accumulation over years
well nigh concedes dementia.
We heard the falcons today.
All these years I thought they were
crows; and the hundred thousand
starlings that fly over our house
every third night, in fact, are crows.
Have you ever listened to Boléro
several times in succession?
This is the clearest path to peace
I know, if done correctly, at night,
with a fine red wine and a fluffy
soft organism nearby. The theme
repeats itself a full eighteen
times, a resplendent opportunity
for fixation, all wordless. Sublime.

Disco Cool

What started disco ended disco.
When the sun was born it was
hot and sweaty. It was blistering.
So God said, let there be cool.
And about 20 millions years later
there was cool (it takes time
to make cool). A multi-faceted
light accelerated toward earth,
landed in the middle of a dance
floor, jumped to the ceiling
and rotated on its axis in gyration
with sound. Men's voices jumped
three octaves and a strange virus
circled the earth causing high
fevers on Saturday nights.
Everything was cool for about ten
years until John Travolta turned cool
into way cool, dance floors cleared
and discos no longer played disco.
Cool started disco, cool kept it going
and too much cool ended it.

Illusionist

I used to read cards and count stones.
Now I'm lucky if I can pick them up.
The world's become an uneasy place
for vagrants and lost souls such as I.
I probably try too hard, or maybe
in ardor, I become lost in sweat.
Do you ever find yourself driving
down roads with nothing but broken
stoplights? Every one is stuck
on yellow, so you make no progress.
It's been years since I've danced.
So long, I can't remember if it's fun
or just a placeholder for the ego.
Familiar faces hide behind weeds.
These friends in animal skins,
do I know them any longer?
Do they know me, elaborator
of visions and implausible explanations?
Old sea warrior, dabbler in mud and tide.

The Universe Grows in Leaps and Bounds

He intoned, with astral pictures and Powerpoint,
a voice behind his face rumbling like an engine.
This was either my college professor in philosophy
or the impish gremlin that kept popping up
in my first-attempts at writing a fantasy novel.
When he paused, mighty waters poured forth.
When he resumed, the waters parted mightily.
All our ears perked and pricked in obeisance.
We all imagined ourselves back in the womb
on Mother Earth's amniotic drip, soul-served
and sealed in the mystical wax of the New Age.
And his hemidemisemiquaver filled one owl's
solitary breath: our ultimate sanctioned good.
But what came through in the end, was his sheer
unbridled surety, coupled with an overwhelmingly
horrific comb-over and a protruding nose.

Clean Slate

I thought I should
let you know
the keys are on
my desk, the money
is in the top
drawer and my
Will is in
a little box
underneath
our bed, marked
Bad Debts,
Liens and Balances Due.

Zen-Heaven

Black widows scraping legs underneath me.
Rattlesnakes in them there hills. And still,
a six by ten foot strip of Astroturf is all I need,
surrounded by blue mountains, obsequious lizards
and a blathering group of blackbirds letting loose.
My daughter says there's no money left for grass.
But my spot faces the sun and the old oaks on the far
canyon wall, zen-heaven for bums like me.
It's 9 AM and I'm already hot, the way it should be.
Ice plants fill up the edges of the courtyard
and spill down the slope, a cool psychological
paradox, and yet I'm told, a frightful nuisance.
Maddie says the gophers come out of little holes
in the early morning, but I haven't seen them.
At night, I remind her, the holes fill up with little
canyon people smoking cigars and drinking tequila.

Limbo

No one can say if this is the end.
Not her doctors, not her daughters,
and certainly not me, a disinterested
party while angels flit by with bedpans
on gossamer, and I in retreat, pinned
to the principle of laissez faire.

She refuses to get out of bed.
What else is new? Mom is dying
because she says she is dying.
She is dying because she heard
it last night on the evening news.

There's nothing like the lure
of a glistening egg, yolk spilling out,
the surrounding white perfection.
Yet now she shuns even the egg,
hitherto the gold standard, hitherto
her mainstay. Where will we be now–
without the lure of the egg?

I've never changed a bedpan.
Fallen angel that I am, mortified
by all manner of the flesh, its ins
and outs and machinations of indecorum.
Yet I am my mother's son, for which
I am all too readily reminded.
Today is peanut butter and jelly day.
Today is the second presidential debate.
CNN chomps at the bit. Mom will love it.

The Right Stuff

She looked up at me from her shovel
and scraggly plastic pink and green
garden gloves with a sprawlingly
cute, though accusatory smile.
Sylvia doesn't think this compost
you bought is very good, she said,
adding that here was a perfect place
to plant bulbs. This got me thinking
about right and wrong, the expediency
of man and the teleology of plants.
My conclusion is documented
in a recent edition of *Botany and the Stars*,
which I have affably dedicated with love
to my dear and industrious wife.

Sadness in a Light Rain

On my way back from the hospital I passed three
bridges, the road just damp enough to reflect light
but not slick enough to injure. Sky dripped a gray
drizzle, wipers barely scraped a view. I counted
only red traffic lights, and there were twenty-three.
I recited nearly all the Gettysburg Address, stumbling
where I always stumble, halfway through, near my poor
power to add or detract. If truth's in the details, then
I have become a slave to lies. If I see what is ahead of me,
I have already lost my way. But if I cry for the wrong
reason or laugh in sadness above my peer's objection,
then I speak a human prayer into the showering gloom.

Third Strike

The last milk dud box
in a bowl at Halloween
buried underneath a sea
of candy corn. A dab
of caramel on vanilla
ice cream, blueberry
pancakes slathered in
fresh whipping cream
conspiring and massing
in your throat. Your mouth
and frontal cortex
want to swing,
but the cerebellum
holds back on principle.

Dialectic

To ward off a fly
without effort, one
needs only good aim;
clearing an eyelash
from a baby's eye
requires all the gentle
precision the universe
can lend. Her quiet
beingness proffers
each breath, expanding
and contracting
like a nascent galaxy,
now death, now life.

Deposition Fare

Receptionist grins behind a beehive.
Dada everywhere on white walls
prefiguring avant-garde outcome.
Ubiquitous bottled water for the saliva
impaired, but nothing quells or quenches.
An hour past starting time and fidgeting
turns tetanus, visions of imprisonment.
First grilling, a cakewalk. The second,
chopped liver with mayonnaise and onion.
Final grilling, red rotisserie with blood
teased drippings. Eight hours, a hog roast
cooked to perfection, medium rare.

The New Me

My eyes followed some bees around our garden
hopping from germander to lavender. Final
conclusion from scientific inquiry: honey bees
prefer germander, but bumble bees like lavender.
I sipped a cold beer in a clear glass mug as the sun
poured down my back and the bees circled me
with vexing caprice. I have a mortal fear of bees.
Once while riding a bicycle, a bee got caught
in my curly hair: I panicked and hit a parked car.
Yet as I age and aches accumulate, I find the bees
get softer. The whole idea of bees is getting softer.

Silent Will

Bless you my son. Bless you my daughter.
Bless all of my dear and faithful friends.
If I hear any whispering I will haunt you.
The sound of your chatter, it reminds me
of crows and frogs and whining trains.
My appetite has left me, or I left it
meandering through these poorly lit halls.
If you brought chocolates, please eat them.
If you brought flowers, please plant them
in the courtyard, if you brought a card,
for heaven's sake don't read it to me.
If I begin to turn blue, don't resuscitate me,
unless I give you the secret sign.

Tangerine on a Train

An orange globe delicately balanced
in one hand; in the other, a smallish
book. Her thumb pressing inward
and rolling down to her last finger
in sequence, round eyes flowing
down the page double-tasking
purpose with autonomic function.
Skin and pith worried open,
the juicy segments acquiesce.
Head tilts on invisible pivot
splitting equal parts pleasure
and concentration, word to mouth
and back to word, beckoning explosive
fruit with a flick of the shoulder
and the slightest nod of approval.

Famous Numbers, and Then There's Me

Avogadro's number, sand and stars, buttons
on the universe's dark coat. Pi's repeating infinitum
unveiling new language based on a circular argument.
Planck and Einstein, big C and little h, humongous
monoliths, broad sequoias shading lesser trees.
Schrodinger's deep equation with Hamiltonian,
the operator promising every lottery player millions.
The Googol, a duotrigintillion, ten thousand sexdecillion
on the long scale, or ten sexdecilliard on the Peletier scale,
numbers black on white as I drift toward sleep.
I see angel hairs splitting the wind and radiant seraphim
lighting the sky. I see unnumbered rays masking
the nascent darkness and portents of ruin.

Edward Nudelman's first full-length poetry collection, *What Looks Like an Elephant*, was published in 2011 by Lummox Press garnering Second Place for the Indie Lit Awards Book of the Year. *Night Fires*, a chapbook published by Pudding House Press in 2009, was a semifinalist for the Journal Award (OSU Press). Nudelman appeared as one of nine poets in the anthology, *Casting the Nines,* in 2009. His poems have recently appeared in *Cortland Review, Valparaiso Review, Chiron Review, Evergreen Review, OCHO, Poets and Artists, Ampersand, Syntax, The Atlanta Review, Mipoesias, Plainsongs, Tears in the Fence, Floating Bridge Press, The Orange Room Review*, and *The Penwood Review*. A cancer research scientist by trade, Nudelman currently owns and operates a rare bookshop in Seattle which he started in 1980.